# A CONCISE CATECHISM FOR CATHOLICS

# *A* CONCISE CATECHISM *for* CATHOLICS

## A SIMPLE EXPOSITION OF CATHOLIC DOCTRINE

Based on the
*Catechism of the Catholic Church*

**Fr. James Tolhurst**

WILLIAM B. EERDMANS PUBLISHING COMPANY
GRAND RAPIDS, MICHIGAN

First published 1993 in the United Kingdom by
Gracewing, Fowler Wright Books
2 Southern Ave., Leominster, Herefordshire HR6 0QF

North American edition published 1993 by
Wm. B. Eerdmans Publishing Co.
255 Jefferson Ave. S.E., Grand Rapids, Michigan 49503


Printed in the United States of America

*Reprinted, December 1993*

IMPRIMI POTEST
Paul Chavasse
STL Provost Cong Orat
21 March 1993

NIHIL OBSTAT
Ieuan Wyn Jones,
Censor

IMPRIMATUR
John Aloysius Ward
OFM Cap,
Archbishop of Cardiff
6 April 1993

The *Nihil Obstat* and *Imprimatur* are a declaration that a book or pamphlet is considered to be free from doctrinal or moral error. It is not implied that those who have granted the *Nihil Obstat* and *Imprimatur* agree with the contents, opinions, or statements expressed.

ISBN 0-8028-0122-6

## CONTENTS

*for GC, AJ/DN, PS, and in memoriam RHT*

# FOREWORD

The years since the Second Vatican Council have seen great developments in the area of Catechetics. In response to the call of the Council, the Church in various parts of the world has re-examined its approach to its catechetical mission and has endeavoured to present its timeless Christian Doctrine in ways that reach the heart and mind of the people of our time. This endeavour will always be a challenge to the Church as the world changes and the means of communication develop.

With all the welcome developments and exciting new approaches, there has been heard in more recent years the suggestion that the formulae of the older form of catechism retain a value which can be most helpful in supplementing the current programmes.

Fr. Tolhurst presents us in this volume with such a catechism. In the question and answer form so familiar to many, he presents the essential teachings of the faith in a clear, comprehensive and comprehensible form. This he effects by drawing on the richness of Sacred Scripture and the Church Fathers and on the documents of the Second Vatican Council.

His work is also designed to present in shorter form Christian Doctrine as now officially presented by the Church in the Universal Catechism of the Catholic Church.

I welcome this work as a valuable contribution to presenting the truth in clarity and fidelity. I am sure it will be welcomed by catechists, students and those who desire an easy-to-use reference book of the Catholic faith.

JOHN MAGEE
BISHOP OF CLOYNE

# FOREWORD TO THE AMERICAN EDITION

Since the close of the Second Vatican Council, renewal of catechesis has been concerned with applying conciliar teachings concretely and faithfully. Most recently, the *Catechism of the Catholic Church* serves, according to Pope John Paul II, as a "very important contribution to the work of renewing the Church's life." It is now the task of all those who value the Church and Her life-giving message to present the Church's timeless faith to the people of our day clearly and joyfully.

The *Catechism of the Catholic Church* is an extensive document, divided into four great pillars: the faith we profess, the faith we celebrate, the faith we live, and the faith we pray. I welcome Father Tolhurst's work as one valuable tool among many in delving into the richness of the *Catechism*. It should become the welcome mainstay of the libraries of catechists, parents, and students at various levels.

One great benefit of Father Tolhurst's *Concise Catechism for Catholics* is its simplicity. In a question and answer format, based on the new catechism, it presents the Church's faith clearly and comprehensively. Moreover, it has the added benefit of facilitating memorization of basic doctrine, basic terminology, prayers, and practices. Thus, in the hands of well-trained catechists, our young people will be given the opportunity both to memorize and to know and understand the content of our faith.

Most Reverend John J. Myers
BISHOP OF PEORIA

# INTRODUCTION

The publication of the *Catechism of the Catholic Church* in 1992, which will soon be issued in an English version, marks the final stage in the program of reform begun by Vatican II thirty years earlier.

But those years have also seen great upheavals and growing uncertainty which have led many to abandon their faith or to doubt its relevance. The various documents emanating from Rome — and in particular those of the pontificate of John Paul II — have shown the Church's awareness of the problem. The *Catechism*, requested by the Synod of Bishops in 1985, is part of a strategy to present the faith in an attractive but totally faithful light to the members of the Church so that by living it they can draw others to its radiance.

This book uses the *Catechism* as its reference, providing paragraph numbers to each question and answer. The format chosen is designed to provide a succinct summary of the 676 pages of the original. It is not a substitute but I hope a worthy companion which is "a compendium of the one and enduring apostolic faith which the Church has guarded and taught through centuries."* May it serve as an hors d'oeuvre especially for those interested in the faith and rather overawed by large volumes.

Feast of St. Joseph, 1993

Joseph Tolhurst
The Oratory
Edgbaston, Birmingham

*Homily of Pope John Paul II, 8 December, 1992

## Abbreviations used in the text

(*Documents with no date are from the Second Vatican Council*)

AA Apostolicam actuositatem (Laity)
AG Ad gentes (Missions)
AH Adversus Haereses of S. Irenaeus († 202)
CA Centesimus annus (1991)
CG City of God of S. Augustine († 430)
CIC Codex iuris canonici: Code of Canon Law
CT Catechesis tradendae (1979)
D Didache (90–100)
DS Denzinger Schönmetzer, *Enchiridion Symbolorum* 35th edition, 1973
DV Dei verbum (Revelation)
GC General Catechetical Directory (1971)
GS Gaudium et spes (The Church in the Modern World)
HV Humanae Vitae (1968)
IS Inter insigniores (1976)
LG Lumen gentium (The Church)
MF Mysterium fidei (1965)
MS Misericordiam suam (1974)
OP Ordo paenitentiae (1974)
PH Personae humanae (1975)
PO Presbyterorum ordinis (Priestly Ministry and Life)
RC De carnis resurrectione: Tertullian († 222/3)
SC Sacrosanctum concilium (Liturgy)
TO XI Council of Toledo (675)
UR Unitatis redintegratio (Ecumenism)

The numerical references on the right of the page refer to the appropriate paragraphs in the New Universal Catechism.

# I

# WE BELIEVE IN ONE GOD

*'The life of man is the vision of God' (A H 4,20,7)*

## Our Desire for God

1. **What is the deepest desire of our nature?**
   We are created with a desire for truth and goodness which comes from God, 'in whom we live and move and have our being' (Acts 17,28). 27ff

2. **How can we come to a knowledge of God?**
   We can come to a knowledge of God through the evidence of creation itself and the voice of our own conscience (Rom 1,19ff) 33ff

3. **What does creation tell us about God?**
   By its unity and structure creation tells us that it comes from a Being of supreme wisdom and love (2 Mac 7;28; Rom 1,19–21) (D V 6) 34.295

4. **Does belief in God contradict the findings of Science?**
   Belief in God, who is Wisdom, cannot contradict the discovery of wisdom in the findings of Science. 159

**5. What is the voice of our conscience?**

It is the awareness that we possess of God's law within our soul: to love and do what is good and avoid what is evil. (GS 16) 1777

**6. What is the soul?**

The soul is the living spiritual principle, created by God to give direction to the human body; by which we possess the seed of eternity. (GS 18) 363

**7. What is the relation of the soul to the body?**

The soul is so intimately united to the body, that it makes the body a living being destined to become in Christ, a Temple of the Spirit. (GS 14) 365

## The Revelation of God

**8. How can we know about the mystery of God Himself?**

We can only know if God makes himself known by his own *revelation* 'for he dwells in unapproachable light'. (I Tim 6;16) (DV 2) 52

**9. Where do we find this revelation?**

We find it uniquely in the Christian Bible. 54ff

**10. Is the Bible merely a sacred book?**

The Bible is the record of God's own communication with mankind. The written word lives and is interpreted by an enduring tradition. (DV 8–9)

**11. What is meant by Tradition?**

Tradition is the handing on of the word of God, revealed in the Old Testament and entrusted in the New Testament to the apostles and their successors. (DV 7) 74ff

**12. What is the Old Testament?**

It is the revelation of God's mind to the People of Israel. 121.201

**13. How did God reveal himself to Israel?**

By his covenant with Abraham (cf. Gen. 15:18) and, through Moses, with the race of Israel (cf. Ex. 24:8), he acquired a people for himself, and to them he revealed himself in words and deeds as the one, true and living God. 145

**14. What do we mean by the inspiration of the Bible?**

We mean that God as the author of Holy Scripture, inspiring human authors freely to understand and write what he wished them to write. (DV 11) 105ff

**15. Does the Old Testament look towards the New?**

The Old Testament attains its full meaning and fulfilment in the New Testament and in turn sheds light upon the New Testament and allows it to be understood more fully. (DV 16)

**16. How does the New Testament fulfil the Old?**

Because it reveals the final Word of God, promised to Israel, Jesus Christ. (Heb 1/2) (DV 2) 124

**17. Will there by any further revelation given to us?**

Jesus is the final and definitive revelation given to us by God, The Beginning and the End. (DV 7; GS 10,45) 66

**18. What does the word Jesus mean?**

The word Jesus literally means 'God saves' or God our Saviour. (Matthew 1,21; 2 Cor 5,19) 430

**19. Why is Jesus called the Word of God?**

Because he is the living mind of God made known to us as man, 'for who has known the mind of God, or who has been his counsellor?' (Rom 11,34)

**20. Why is Jesus called Christ or Messiah?**

Because he was *anointed* (= Christos) by God the Father for the salvation and redemption of the human race. (Acts 10,38) 436ff

**21. Why did Jesus need to redeem the human race?**

Because of the disobedience to God which we call sin.

## Original Sin

**22. When did sin enter the world?**

Sin entered the world at the beginning, the dawn of history. (GS 13) 390

**23. What was this sin called?**

Original Sin, because it was committed at the origin of the human race.
(Gen 3,6; Rom 5,12)

**24. What is Original Sin?**

The loss of that perfect holiness in which God made us, and of perfect union of mind and heart with Him. 399ff

**25. What was the consequence of Original Sin?**

A wounded nature which was passed down to all mankind, and a loss of God's friendship. (Rom 5,12)

**26. Have we all been born with Original Sin?**

All have been born with Original Sin except the Blessed Virgin Mary, who alone was preserved by God and conceived without sin. (LG 56)

**27. Why was the Virgin Mary preserved from Original Sin?**

Because he who would be born of her would be the Son of God: (Lk 1,35) (LG 61) 'that pure womb which He himself made to be pure'. (AH 4.33.11)

**28. What is this privileged state called?**

The Immaculate Conception. 490

**29. Why did the Son of God need a sinless mother?**

Because he who would be born of her was truly God and truly man, in whom there could be no sin.

# II
# WE BELIEVE IN ONE LORD JESUS CHRIST

## The Incarnation of the Son of God

**30. What do we call the birth of Jesus?**

We call the birth of Jesus the *Incarnation* because 'the Word was *made flesh* and dwelt among us'. (John I,14 cf. I Tim 3,16)

**31. Was Jesus born of a virgin mother?**

Jesus was born of a virgin mother. Mary was, and ever remained a virgin, full of grace and the most blessed among women. (LG 63) 499

**32. Had Jesus a human father?**

Jesus had no human father because he was the Son of God. 503

**33. Where and when was Jesus born?**

Jesus was born in a stable in Bethlehem, the city of David, in the reign of Caesar Augustus (Luke 2,1). 525

## Jesus, the Son of God

**34. Is Jesus truly God?**

Jesus is truly God for 'in him lives divinity in all its fullness'. (Col 2,9) (AG 3)

**35. Why is Jesus truly God?**

He is truly God because he is the Son of God with one and the same being as God the Father. 465

**36. How do we know that Jesus is truly God?**

We know that Jesus is truly God from his words, his works and his life.

**37. How does Jesus speak of His Divinity?**

Jesus speaks clearly of his Divinity when he says 'I and the Father are one' (John 10,30), 'Believe me that I am in the Father and the Father in me' (John 14,11), 'Before Abraham was, I am.' (Jn 8,58), and in his reply to the High Priest. (Lk 22,70) 441ff

**38. How does Jesus show by his life that He is God?**

He shows by his life that he is God because nobody but God could do the works that he did during his life: curing the sick, the blind, forgiving sinners, raising the dead; and could rise from His own grave after he had been put to death. (Acts 10;38–40)

## Jesus, Truly Man

**39. Is Jesus truly man?**

Jesus is truly man, the son of the Virgin Mary.

**40. How do we know that Jesus is truly man?**

We know that Jesus is truly man from his life on earth which is recorded in the New Testament.

**41. What does the New Testament tell us about the humanity of Christ?**

It tells us that he became tired (John 4,6), hungry (Luke 4,2), thirsty (John 4,7), he was filled with compassion (Matthew 15,32), he loved His friends (John 11,5), was sorrowful even to death (Mark 14,34), was bathed in a sweat of blood (Luke 22,44) and finally suffered the pain of scourging and crucifixion. (Phil 2,8) (GS 22)

**42. How can Jesus be both God and man?**

Jesus can be both God and man because he is one Person, God the Son, the Word, who took to himself our human nature. 470

**43. Was Jesus God from the moment of his incarnation?**

Jesus was always God; and was God made man from the moment of his incarnation: 'In the beginning was the Word . . . and the Word was God . . . and the Word was made flesh.' (John 1,1.14 cf. 1 Tim 3,16)

**44. Did Jesus always know that he was the Son of God?**

Jesus always knew he was the Son of God for he said 'He who sent me is with me; He has not left me alone;' and 'I and the Father are one.' (John 8,29; 10,30) 473

**45. Was Jesus subject to sin?**

Jesus because he was truly man took on the limitations of our human nature but not sin nor those weaknesses derived from sin which are not natural to our nature: 'Like us in all things but sin'. (Heb 4:15) 603

## Jesus, our Redeemer

**46. What do we call the chief sufferings of Jesus?**

We call the chief sufferings of Jesus, his Passion and Death.

**47. Why did Christ suffer his Passion?**

Christ suffered his Passion because of our sins and his great love for us.
(I Cor 15,3; Eph 1,7.) (SC 5) 604ff

**48. Why is Jesus called our Redeemer?**

Because He offered himself even to death for us, to unite us once more with God our Father, by dying he destroyed our death, by rising he restored our life.

**49. Where did Jesus die?**

Jesus died on a cross on Calvary, outside the city of Jerusalem. (Lk 23,33)

**50. Why do we make the sign of the cross?**

We make the sign of the cross to remind ourselves that through the passion and cross of Christ we come to share in the life of the Trinity through our baptism, and our life of grace.

## God is Unity in Trinity

**51. In making the sign of the cross, how are we reminded of the Trinity?**

We are reminded of the Trinity by the words we use when we make the sign of the cross: *In the Name of the Father and of the Son, and of the Holy Spirit.*

**52. Is there only one God?**

There is only one God, He who is Truth and Love. (Ex 3,14) 212ff

**53. Why do we believe that there are three Persons in one God?**

We believe because Jesus is the Son of God sent by the Father and conceived by the Holy Spirit, who as Trinity come to make their home in us. (Jn 14,23) 240ff

**54. Are these three Persons, three gods?**

These three Persons are not three gods; 'we distinguish the Persons: we do not divide the Godhead'. (TO)

**55. What is the relationship of the Son to the Father?**

The Son proceeds within the being of the Father from all eternity, as his Word: the image of the invisible God. (Col 1:15)

**56. What is the relationship between the Holy Spirit and the Father and the Son?**

The Holy Spirit proceeds from the Father and the Son with whom he is worshipped and glorified, as the outpouring of their love from all eternity. 689ff

**57. Can the mind of man form an image of the Trinity?**

Man alone is able to speak his word within himself: 'I *know* myself'. Also, in knowing, man possesses that knowledge in *love*. This is an image of the Trinity.

## Jesus, Source of Life and Wisdom

**58. Why do we call Jesus, the new Adam?**

Because as all men find their origin in the first man, Adam; so they are united in Jesus, the new Adam: 'as in Adam all die, so also in Christ shall all be made alive'. (I Cor 15,22) 775

**59. How is all mankind united in Jesus?**

Because communion between men is rooted in communion with God through the Church. (GS 24.42) 1939

**60. What are the marks of this union in Jesus Christ?**

The marks of this union are perfect communion in charity and in the truth of the Word of God: 'they remained faithful to the teaching of the apostles . . . united heart and soul'. (Acts 2,42; 4,32).

# III
# WE BELIEVE IN ONE HOLY CATHOLIC AND APOSTOLIC CHURCH

## We have only one Teacher, the Christ

**61. How is the Church united in the truth?**

The Church is united in the truth because the Church has 'only one Teacher, the Christ' (Matthew 23,10) who is Truth itself. (LG 12)

**62. How does Christ teach the Church?**

Christ teaches the Church in the same way that God taught the people of the Old Testament, through their spiritual leaders and teachers. 62ff

**63. Who did Christ choose to teach the truth of his Gospel?**

Christ chose the twelve apostles. (SC 6)

## The Pope and the Bishops

**64. How do we know that Christ chose Peter and the Apostles?**

Because we are told in the Gospel that he chose twelve of his disciples and named them apostles, giving them his authority. (Matthew 10,2–4; Mark, 3,13–19; Luke 6, 13–17; Acts 1,13) 858

**65. Did Christ make Peter the head of His Church?**

Christ chose Simon and changed his name to Peter, making him head of the Church. (LG 19)

**66. How do we know that Peter was made head of Christ's Church?**

Because he said to him: 'You are Peter and on this rock I will build my Church and the powers of hell shall not prevail against it. I will give you the keys of the kingdom of heaven and whatever you bind on earth shall be bound in heaven, and whatever you loose on earth shall be loosed in heaven'. (Matthew 16, 18–20) 881

**67. Does Christ still teach His Church?**

Christ still teaches his Church through the successors of Peter and the apostles, the Pope and the Bishops. (LG 22.25) 861

**68. What is the universal power of the Pope in the Church?**

The Pope as Roman pontiff and successor of Peter has universal power to proclaim the truth of God and strengthen the Church: 'Simon, Simon, behold Satan demanded to have you all that he might sift you like wheat, but I have prayed for you that your faith may not fail; and when you have come to yourself, strengthen your brethren.' (Luke 22, 31–33) 891

**69. Can the Pope err when he acts with the fulness of Christ's authority?**

The Pope cannot err when he acts with the fulness of Christ's authority defining a teaching concerning faith or morals to be held by the whole Church. He is infallible because Christ in whose name He is speaking cannot err. (LG 25)

**70. What union exists between the Bishops and the Pope?**

The Bishops are united to the Pope, because just as by Christ's will Peter and the other apostles constituted one apostolic college under Christ, so in a similar way do the Pope and the Bishops teaching in communion with him. (LG 23) 883

## IV
## THE CHURCH UNITED BY CHRIST IN ONE LIFE THROUGH THE SACRAMENTS

**71. Do all the members of the Church share in the life of Christ?**

All the members of the Church do share in the life of Christ for they and He are one body 'though many members'. (I Corinthians 12,12). (LG 4) 1140

**72. How do all the members share in the one life of Christ?**

They share in the one life of Christ through the Sacraments and prayer. (SC 12)

**73. What is a Sacrament?**

A Sacrament is a visible sign of an invisible grace ordained by Jesus Christ. (LG 3; SC 5) 1131

**74. What is grace?**

Grace is a share in the very life of God, through which we can know and love him and call him our Father: 'Because you are sons, God has sent the spirit of His Son into our hearts, crying Abba! Father!' (Galatians 4,6) 1996ff

**75. How many Sacraments are there?**

There are seven Sacraments: Baptism, Confirmation, Holy Eucharist, Penance, Anointing of the Sick, Holy Orders and Matrimony.

**76. How do the Sacraments differ from other visible signs and sacramentals?**

The Sacraments not only signify but also cause grace because they are the actions of Christ himself. (SC 7.56) 1127

**77. What are Sacramentals?**

Objects and actions whose effects depend on the faith and devotion of the person using them, and the approval of the Church for their use. These include Holy Water, the Rosary, Benediction and Stations of the Cross. 1667ff

## V
## THE SACRAMENTS OF CHRISTIAN INITIATION: BAPTISM, CONFIRMATION, THE HOLY EUCHARIST

### Baptism: A Rising to Life in Christ

**78. What is Baptism?**

Baptism is the Sacrament by which we are reborn to God, cleansed from original sin and personal sins and made a member of the Church. 1227 1263

**79. How do we know that Christ instituted Baptism?**

We know that he instituted Baptism from these words: 'Go therefore and make disciples of all nations, baptising them in the Name of the Father, and of the Son, and of the Holy Spirit' (Matthew, 28,19) and by its practice in the early Church. (Acts 2,41; 8,13.38; 10,48ff).

**80. Who can baptize?**

Baptism is usually given by a priest or deacon but anyone may baptize in case of necessity. 1256

**81. How is Baptism given?**

Baptism is given by pouring water on the head of the one being baptized, saying at the same time: 'I baptize you in the Name of the Father, and of the Son and of the Holy Spirit.'

**82. Is Baptism necessary for all men to be saved?**

Baptism is necessary, for Jesus Himself said 'Unless a man is born again through water and the Spirit, he cannot enter the kingdom of God'. (John 3,5) 1257

**83. Is Baptism by water necessary for all?**

Baptism by water is not necessary for all. Those, who through no fault of their own cannot be baptized with water, may enter the kingdom of God through the Baptism of desire or of blood.

**84. What is Baptism of desire or of blood?**

Catechumens and those who accept death out of love of God are said to receive the fruits of baptism 'by desire' or 'in their blood'. (Acts 17,23; Mt 2,16–18; Jn 15,13) 1258

**85. What does the Church teach about children who die before baptism?**

The Church believes that God does not abandon those who die in innocence, and responds to her prayers on their behalf. (Mk 10:14; Jn 15,13) 1261

**86. Are separated Christians members of Christ?**

All those who have been truly baptized are our brethren and members of Christ even though their union with the Body of Christ is incomplete. (UR 22) 1271

## Confirmation: The Completion of Baptism

**87. What is Confirmation?**

Confirmation is the Sacrament by which those who are born again in Baptism receive the seal of the Holy Spirit, the gift of the Father and the Son.

**88. Is Confirmation distinct from Baptism?**

Confirmation brings the Sacrament of Baptism to completion. We see in the Acts of the Apostles that the Apostles laid hands on those who had been baptized so that they would receive the Holy Spirit. (Acts 8,14; 19,5) 1289

**89 Does Confirmation bestow a likeness to Christ?**

Confirmation does bestow a likeness to Christ which we call a *character* because the Christian, having been born again in Christ now takes on the fullness of that likeness through the gift of the Holy Spirit. 1295–6

**90. Is Confirmation the source of the Christian apostolate?**

Confirmation is the source of the Christian apostolate because the Christian is anointed with holy oil to live in the world and bear witness to the faith he has received, even to the shedding of his blood. (LG 11; AA 3; AG 11) 1303

**91. Who is the ordinary minister of Confirmation?**

The ordinary minister of Confirmation is a Bishop, the successor of the apostles, but priests can confirm in certain circumstances, as for instance when they receive an adult into full communion. (LG 11) 1312

## The Holy Eucharist: The Abiding Presence of Christ

**92. What is the Sacrament of the Holy Eucharist?**

The Sacrament of the Holy Eucharist is Jesus Christ himself, true God and true man under the appearances of bread and wine as our *thanksgiving and praise* (= Eucharist). The source and summit of the Christian life. (SC 10) 1355

**93. Did Christ promise to give himself in this way?**

He did promise to give himself in this way when he said 'I am the bread of life which came down from heaven ... As the living Father sent me and I live because of the Father, so he who eats me will live because of me and the bread which I shall give for the life of the world is my flesh. (John 6, 51.57)

**94. When did Christ fulfil this promise?**

When he took bread and wine into his hands at the Last Supper and changed them into His Body and Blood. (SC 47) 1339ff

**95. Do we believe that Christ becomes really and substantially present in the Holy Eucharist or Mass?**

We do believe that Christ becomes really and substantially present by the changing of the entire reality of bread and wine into His Body and Blood. (MF 39)

**96. Do bread and wine remain after this real change?**

Bread and wine do not remain after this real change but only the appearances of bread and wine. 1374

**97. How does the Church describe the change that takes place?**

The Church describes it with the word *Transubstantiation* which means an entire conversion of the bread and wine into the Body and Blood of Christ. (M F 46) 1376

**98. Do we receive the true Body and Blood of Jesus Christ in the Holy Eucharist?**

We receive Christ's Body and Blood, our Lord and our God in the Holy Eucharist.

**99. When does Christ become present?**

Christ becomes present when the priest pronounces the words of *consecration* over the bread and wine during the Eucharistic Prayer through the action of the Holy Spirit. (MF 34) 1353

**100. Does Christ continue to be present after the consecration?**

Christ continues to be present as long as the appearances of bread and wine remain, as our Lord and our God. (MF 11.56) 1377

**101. Why is the Holy Eucharist also called Holy Communion?**

Because when we receive Jesus Christ in the Holy Eucharist we are united by him into one Body 'That they may all be one; even as You Father are in Me and I am in You, may they be one in Us.' (John 17,21) (LG 7)

**102. Does the Church wish us to receive Holy Communion frequently?**

The Church wishes us to receive Holy Communion every day if possible for Jesus has told us 'he who eats my flesh and drinks my blood abides in me and I in him.' (John 6,56) We may even receive Communion twice in the same day during the celebration of the Holy Eucharist. (CIC 917) 1389

**103. What is necessary to receive Holy Communion worthily?**

We should keep the Eucharistic fast* and not be conscious of having committed grave sin, humbly recalling the faith of the centurion: 'Lord, I am not worthy to receive you, only say the word and I shall be healed'. (Cf. Mt 8,8) (CIC 919) 1385ff

* One hour before the time of receiving Communion; water does not break the fast.

**104. May Catholics share in the Eucharist of other Christian communities?**

Catholics may not share in the Eucharist of other Christian communities because the Holy Eucharist is the expression of perfect unity already achieved in faith, in hope and in love. (U R 8; CIC 923) 1399

**105. What is the Church's attitude to other Christian communities?**

The Church prays that all Christians who are deprived of the fullness of belief, teaching and Sacraments may one day be gathered 'at a single celebration of the Eucharist in the one and only Church'. (UR 4) 1400

**106. Are we bound to give Divine worship to the Holy Eucharist?**

We are bound to worship the Holy Eucharist because in this Sacrament Jesus Christ is truly Emmanuel, 'God with us'. (MF 67)

**107. How do we worship the Holy Eucharist?**

We worship the Holy Eucharist by visiting the Church and genuflecting before the tabernacle, by saying 'Amen' when we receive the Body of Christ in Holy Communion and by other Eucharistic devotions such as Benediction. (MF 66) 1379

**108. What is Benediction?**

Benediction is a public act of worship in which the Holy Eucharist is removed from the tabernacle and after Exposition is raised in blessing (= Benediction) over the people.

**109. Is Christ present under either the appearances of bread or wine?**

Christ is wholly present under either appearance. (DS 930–2) 1390

## Christ our Sacrifice

**110. Why did Jesus will to become present under the appearances of bread and wine?**

Because Jesus willed to offer Himself in sacrifice as bread of life and life-giving blood, shed for us. (Jn. 6,55–6)

**111. What is a Sacrifice?**

A Sacrifice is an act of love and worship by which we enter into full communion with God and honour Him as Lord of all. 1368

**112. Does a sacrifice involve the shedding of blood?**

Not every sacrifice involves the shedding of blood but the supreme sacrifice of love and worship will involve the gift of oneself even to the shedding of blood: 'Greater love has no man than this, that a man lay down his life for his friends.' (John 15,13)

**113. How is the Holy Eucharist a sacrifice?**

Because it is the very Body of Christ offered up to unite man to God 'by that will we have been sanctified through the offering of the Body of Jesus Christ once for all'. (Hebrews 10,10). 1362

**114. How do we know that the Holy Eucharist is a true sacrifice?**

We know that the Holy Eucharist is a true sacrifice from the context of the Last Supper, the Passover and the words used by Jesus 'This cup which is poured out for you is the new covenant in my Blood' (Luke 22,20) as well as the constant teaching of the Church that 'Christ our passover lamb has been sacrificed'. (I Corinthians 5,7). 1365

**115. Is each Mass a true sacrifice?**

Each Mass is a true sacrifice because through the person of the priest the risen Christ who dies no more offers himself until he comes again in glory. (I Cor 11,26) 1369

# VI
# THE SACRAMENTS OF HEALING: PENANCE AND THE ANOINTING OF THE SICK

## Penance: Sacrament of God's forgiveness

**116. What is the Sacrament of Penance (or Reconciliation)**

Penance (or Reconciliation) is the Sacrament of God's merciful forgiveness for those sins committed after Baptism. 1425ff

**117. Why is the Sacrament known as Reconciliation or Confession?**

Because in confessing our sins we are reconciled to the Church also. (PO 5) (LG 11) 1444

**118. Is sorrow necessary for Confession?**

We must not only be sorry for our sins which have offended God who has loved us but we must also resolve to lead a better life in the future. 1450ff

**119. How can we express such sorrow for sin?**

We can say such prayers as:

> O my God because you are so good, I am very sorry that I have sinned against you, and by the help of your grace I will not sin again.
>
> Lord, Jesus, Son of God, have mercy on me, a sinner.

**120. Does sorrow motivated purely by love of God forgive sins?**

Sorrow for love of God does forgive our sins even before we confess them, although if they are mortal we are bound to confess them as soon as possible. 1452

**121. What is mortal sin?**

A grave violation of the law of God committed deliberately, knowing it to be wrong. 1859

**122. Why must we confess every mortal sin to a priest?**

Because every mortal sin offends God and wounds his Church and 'he imparts His forgiveness by means of the Church and through the ministry of the priest.' (OP 6) 1456

**123. When did Christ give priests the power to forgive sins?**

When he breathed on his apostles who possessed the fullness of the priesthood and said 'Receive the Holy Spirit. If you forgive the sins of any, they are forgiven; if you retain the sins of any, they are retained.' (John 20,22) 1444

**124. How does a priest forgive sins?**

A priest forgives sins by listening to a person's confession, giving him a penance and absolving him in the Name of the Trinity. 1456

**125. What are the words of absolution?**

The words of absolution are: 'God the Father of mercies, through the death and resurrection of His Son has reconciled the world to himself and sent the Holy Spirit among us for the forgiveness of sins; through the ministry of the Church may God give you pardon and peace, and I absolve you from your sins in the Name of the Father, and of the Son and of the Holy Spirit.'

**126. Why does the priest give a penance?**

Because genuine conversion implies a desire to make reparation for sins committed, a penance is both a remedy for sin and an aid to a renewal of life. (MS 6) 1459ff

**127. What is the origin of the penance?**

Originally the Church, conscious of the evil of sin, insisted on strict acts of penance, but she now allows prayers, fasting and good deeds to be joined to the merits of Christ, Our Lady and the Saints to take their place, which she terms indulgences. 1434

**128. What is an Indulgence?**

An indulgence is a prayer or good deed which the Church enriches by the merits of Christ and the Communion of Saints to make reparation for our sins. It can also be applied to those who are in Purgatory. 1471ff

**129. Why should we go to Confession when we have not commited mortal sin?**

Because we receive advice and help from the priest, habits of sin are overcome and we increase in humility and love for God and the members of the Church. 1458

**130. How often are we bound to go to Confession?**

We are bound to confess serious sins at least once a year. (CIC 989)

**131. Why should children make their first Confession before Holy Communion?**

Because children have the right to turn to Jesus in Confession and to ask him to forgive their faults and help them to increase in love for him whom they are soon to receive in Holy Communion. (GC 5; CIC 914)

## The Anointing of the Sick: The Healing of Christ

**132. What is the Sacrament of the Anointing of the Sick?**

The Sacrament of The Anointing of the Sick is that same action of Christ himself towards those who were sick when he cured them and forgave them their sins. (Mk 2,5.9) 1503

**133. By what authority does the Church regard The Anointing of the Sick as a Sacrament?**

The Church regards The Anointing of the Sick as a Sacrament on the authority of Christ who sent the apostles to heal the sick (Mk 6,13) and of St James who says 'If one of you is sick, he should send for the elders of the Church, and they must anoint him with oil in the name of the Lord and pray over him. The prayer of faith will save the sick man and the Lord will raise him up again; if he has committed sins, he will be forgiven.' (James 5,13–16) 1511

**134. Is The Anointing of the Sick only for those at the point of death?**

It is not only for those at the point of death but for any who are in danger of death from sickness or old age. (SC 73; CIC 1004) 1523

**135. What words does the priest use in The Anointing of the Sick?**

The priest says as he anoints the forehead: 'Through this holy anointing may the Lord in his love and mercy help you with the grace of the Holy Spirit.' Then, as he anoints the hands he says 'May the Lord, who frees you from sin, save you and raise you up. Amen.'

**136. What are the effects of the Sacrament of The Anointing of the Sick?**

The effects of the Sacrament of The Anointing of the Sick are to comfort and strengthen the sick person, to remit sin and anxiety about illness and death, and even to restore health if this is God's will. 1520ff

# VII
# THE SACRAMENTS OF THE CONSECRATED STATE: HOLY ORDERS AND MATRIMONY

## Holy Orders: The ministry of Christ's priesthood

**137. What is the Sacrament of Holy Orders?**

The Sacrament of Holy Orders is the Sacrament by which men receive the power to be ministers of Jesus Christ, as bishops, priests and deacons. 1554

**138. When did Jesus institute Holy Orders?**

When he instituted the Sacrament of the Holy Eucharist, saying to his apostles: 'Do this in memory of me'. (Luke 22,19) (SC47) 611

**139. Do all members of the Church share in the priesthood of Christ?**

All members share in the royal priesthood of Christ through their Baptism (I Peter 2,9) but those who have received the Sacrament of Holy Orders are chosen from among men by a special vocation and an unique power over the Body and Blood of Christ. (LG 10) 1547

**140. Why is celibacy in harmony with the priesthood?**

Because it is the generous choice of the personal way of life of Christ on earth; a way which allows a man to give himself to all while being devoted to God alone. (Matthew 19:12) (PO 16) 1579

**141. Can women receive the priesthood?**

Women cannot receive the priesthood because the priest manifests the ministry of Christ's priesthood in his own person and Christ was and remains a man; and chose only men as his apostles. (IS 5; CIC 1024) 1577

**142. Do Holy Orders confer an abiding relationship to Christ?**

Holy Orders do confer an abiding relationship or *character*, for Christ's priesthood continues for ever. (Hebrews 7,24). 1582

**143. How do priests act in the person of Christ?**

Priests act in the person of Christ primarily by offering the Sacrifice of the Mass, the Holy Eucharist, but also by administering the Sacrament of Penance and The Anointing of the Sick, even if they are personally unworthy. 1584

**144. Does the worthiness of the minister affect the power of the sacraments?**

A priest's unworthiness or sinfulness cannot prevent the action of Christ in the sacraments. 1584

**145. Is it fitting for people to give money to the priest for Mass and the administration of the Sacraments?**

It is fitting for people to give money to the priest as they did in the Old Testament: 'the ministers serving in the Temple get their food from the Temple and those serving at the altar can claim their share from the altar itself.'
(I Corinthians 9, 13–14) (CIC 945)

## Matrimony: A Lifelong Union in Christ

**146. What is the Sacrament of Matrimony?**

The Sacrament of Matrimony is the Sacrament which blesses the lifelong union of man and woman. A union which reflects that of Christ's union with the Church. 1612ff

**147. Who are the ministers of the Sacrament of Matrimony?**

The Ministers of the Sacrament of Matrimony are the spouses themselves. 1623

**148. What is the part of the priest or deacon in the Sacrament of Matrimony?**

The priest or deacon must witness the marriage on behalf of the Church and bless the married couple. 1630

**149. How do we know that Matrimony is a Sacrament?**

From the constant teaching of the Church based on the words of Saint Paul 'This is a great *mystery* (= Sacrament) and I mean in reference to Christ and the Church'. (Ephesians 5,32). 1616

**150. What are the effects of the Sacrament of Matrimony?**

The Sacrament of Matrimony enables husband and wife to give themselves undividedly to each other and 'to cooperate with the love of God their Creator who through them will enlarge the human family'. (GS 50) 1638ff

**151. Does such undivided love between husband and wife allow divorce?**

It cannot allow of divorce because of Christ's undivided union with the Church of which marriage itself is an effective sign: 'What therefore God has joined together, let no man put asunder.'
(Matthew 19,6; Mk 10:1ff) (GS 47) 1644

**152. What is the difference between a divorce and an annulment?**

A decree of annulment declares that in fact there was no marriage from the beginning, whereas a divorce takes place between two people who are truly married.

**153. What is a mixed marriage?**

A marriage in which only one of the partners is a Catholic.

**154. Why does the Church impose conditions in the case of a mixed marriage?**

The Church is aware of the danger of religious indifference and probable conflict over the duty of the baptism and education of children in the Catholic faith. 1633

**155. What conditions does the Church impose before allowing a mixed marriage?**

The Church demands of Catholic partners that they should be prepared to remove all dangers of falling away from the faith and make a sincere promise to have all the children baptised and brought up in the Catholic Church; and that the other party is fully aware of this obligation. (CIC 1125) 1635

**156. How must husband and wife cooperate with God's creative love in enlarging the human family?**

They must allow each and every marriage act to remain open to the transmission of human life. (HV 11) 1652

**157. To whom does it belong to decide how many children a husband and wife should have?**

It belongs to the parents themselves and nobody else to decide in God's sight and according to His laws the number of their children. 2372

**158. Does the law of God forbid artificial means of birth control?**

The law of God does forbid artificial means of birth control because these deliberately exclude the transmission of human life. 2370

**159. Does recourse to the infertile period conflict with the love of husband and wife?**

Recourse to the infertile period does not conflict with their love but rather allows them to show their affection in the practice of a certain restraint, so giving proof of a truly authentic love. (HV 16) 2370

**160. Why does the Church esteem perfect chastity above marriage?**

Because those who accept perfect chastity for the sake of the kingdom of heaven (Matthew 9,12) bear a more perfect witness to that greater love of Christ of which marriage itself is also a sign. (LG 42) 1619

# VIII
# PRAYER

## What Prayer is?

**161. What is prayer?**

Prayer is the lifting up of the mind and heart to God in love. 2559

**162. How should we pray?**

We should pray always through Christ Our Lord, both in private and in union with the members of Christ's Body the Church. (SC 2–5)

**163. Why should we pray in private?**

Because Jesus often prayed to the Father in private (Mark 1,35; 6,46; Luke 6,12; 9,18) and told us: 'When you pray, go into your room and shut the door and pray to your Father in secret' (Matthew 6,6) (SC 12) 2602

**164. Do we have a pattern for our prayer?**

We have a pattern for our prayer in the *Our Father* taught us by Christ Himself. (See appendix) 2759ff

## The Whole Church United in Prayer

**165. What do we call the public prayer of the Church?**

We call the public prayer of the Church, the Sacred Liturgy. (SC 2)

**166. What are the essential acts of the Liturgy?**

The essential acts of the Liturgy are The Holy Eucharist, The Sacraments and the Liturgy of the Hours. 1174ff

**167. Why should we take part in the Liturgy?**

Because in it we are united with Christ and with each other in one hymn of praise to God Our Father: 'They occupied themselves continually with the apostles' teaching, and fellowship, the breaking of bread, and the fixed times of prayer.' (Acts 2,42) (SC 8) 1108

**168. What is the Communion of Saints?**

It is the union of all the members of the Church in heaven, on earth and in purgatory as one family in Jesus Christ. (LG 50) 957ff

**169. Why is Our Lady a unique member of the Communion of Saints?**

Because she brought forth the Son of God who is the 'first-born among many brethren'. (Romans 8,29) (LG 62)

**170. Can we call Our Lady, Mother of the Church?**

We can call Our Lady Mother of the Church because in giving birth to Christ, she became a mother of those who would be reborn in Him. (GS 65; SC 103) 967

**171. Are we right to honour Mary and pray to her?**

We are right to honour Mary, for in honouring her and praying to her we honour The Father Who chose her to be the mother of His only Son. 971

**172. What is the chief prayer to Our Lady that the Church uses?**

The chief prayer to Our Lady which the Church uses is the *Hail Mary*. (see appendix)

**173. What do we mean by the Assumption of Mary into heaven?**

We mean that at the end of her life, because of her perfect holiness, she was taken up to heaven, body and soul by the power of God. (LG 59) 966

# IX
# THE LAW OF CHRIST

## The Commandments: The Love of God and Our Neighbour

**174. How do we show that we love God?**

We show that we love God by keeping his commandments, for Christ said: 'If you keep my commandments, you will abide in my love'. (John 15,10).

**175. What are the commandments of Christ?**

The commandments of God were given to Israel through the teaching of Moses and brought to perfection by Christ, especially in the Sermon on the Mount. (Matthew ch. 5–8) 1966ff

**176. What are the Commandments given to Israel?**

Ten Commandments were given to Israel:

1. I am the Lord Your God. You shall have no other gods besides me.
2. You shall not take the Name of the Lord, Your God in vain.
3. Remember to keep holy the Sabbath day.
4. Honour your father and your mother.
5. You shall not kill.
6. You shall not commit adultery.
7. You shall not steal.
8. You shall not bear false witness against your neighbour.

9. You shall not covet your neighbour's wife.
10. You shall not covet anything that belongs to your neighbour.

(Ex 20; Dt 5)

## 1st Commandment: Belief in God

**177. What is the first commandment?**

I am the Lord Your God. You shall have no other gods besides me.

**178. What does the first commandment demand of us?**

We must believe in God, hope in him and love in him above all others and worship him alone. (Mt 4,10) 2095

**179. How do we show our belief in God?**

We show our belief in God by making acts of faith, by praying for an increase of faith, and by studying our religion so that we can put its teachings into practice. (CT 25) 2088

**180. What is an act of faith?**

An act of faith is one like the following:

My God, I believe in you and all your Church teaches, because you have said it and your word is true.

**181. How do we worship God?**

We worship God by putting Him first in our thoughts, words and actions, 'paying him the homage of our faith'. (Rom 1,5)

**182. Why do we respect the statues and pictures of Christ, Our Lady, and the Saints?**

We respect such statues and pictures to show them honour even as men think it right to respect the images of the great figures of this world. They are our cloud of witnesses (Heb 12,1) encouraging us to pray. 1161

**183. How do we show that we hope in God?**

We show that we hope in God when we will what God wills for us; for 'our heavenly Father knows our needs.' (Matthew 6,32) 2090

**184. How do we sin against the first commandment?**

We sin against the first commandment, when we do not pray or give honour to God; deny our belief in Him or by any sort of idolatry.

**185. How does a person sin by idolatry?**

A person sins by idolatry, when he gives someone or something created the honour that is due to God alone, as in gross superstition, recourse to astrology, the occult, or the service of Satan. 2110ff

**186. Is Satan or the Devil a real person?**

Satan (= the adversary) is a real person who defied God. He and the other fallen angels direct their hatred especially towards mankind. (Rev 12,17) 391ff

**187. How do we know that Satan exists?**

We know that Satan exists from the words of Christ who mentions his fall from grace, and calls him the prince of this world and the father of lies, who is cursed for all eternity (Luke 10,18; John 14,30; 8,44; Matthew 24,41); also from the constant teaching of the Church. 391ff

**188. What should be our attitude towards Satan?**

We should see him as part of the great mystery of sin and its impact, and 'resist him firm in our faith' (1 Peter 5,9), trusting in God and his angels and the sacramentals of the Church to protect us. 334

## 2nd and 8th Commandments: Speaking the Truth

**189. What are the second and eighth commandments?**

The second commandment is 'You shall not take the Name of the Lord Your God in vain'. The eighth commandment is 'You shall not bear false witness against your neighbour.'

**190. What do the second and eighth commandments demand of us?**

We must bear witness to the truth towards God and towards our neighbour.

**191. How do we sin against the second commandment?**

We sin against the second commandment by going against what we have vowed or promised to God; by perjury and blasphemy. 2147ff

**192. Have we a duty to keep our word?**

As followers of Christ who is the Truth we should be known for our truthfulness: 'Let what you say be simply 'Yes' or 'No'' (Matthew 5,37; James 5,12). The martyr is the supreme witness to the truth.

**93. How do we sin against the eighth commandment?**

We sin against the eighth commandment when by lying, rash judgment, calumny or detraction, we take away the good name of our neighbour.

## 3rd Commandment: Keeping Sunday Holy

**194. What is the third commandment?**

The Third commandment is 'Remember to keep holy the Sabbath day'.

**195. What does the third commandment demand of us?**

We must keep Sunday holy, as well as the feast days of obligation laid down by the Church. (CIC 1246) 1166 2180

**196. Why do we keep Sunday holy?**

Because Sunday is the new Sabbath which Christ made holy by his Resurrection. 2174

**197. How do we keep Sunday holy?**

We keep Sunday holy principally by participating in the Holy Eucharist, and using the day to rest in, and with God. (CIC 1247) 2184

## 4th Commandment: Respect for Authority

**198. What is the fourth commandment?**

The fourth commandment is 'Honour your father and your mother'.

**199. What does the fourth commandment demand of us?**

We must obey our parents and our lawful superiors in the reasonable exercise of their authority. (Rom 1,28–31; I Pt 2;13ff) 2199

**200. What are the duties of a citizen towards his country?**

A citizen must contribute to the welfare of his country by using his vote, paying taxes, defending his country's rights when necessary, and by playing his full part in society. (GS 75) 2238ff

**201. What are the duties of lawful authorities?**

They must be just in the exercise of their authority, realising that all authority comes from God (John 19,11), and they must protect the rights of the individual while promoting the good of the whole community. 2234ff

## 5th Commandment: The Sacredness of Human Life

**202. What is the fifth commandment?**

The fifth commandment is 'You shall not kill'.

**203. What does the fifth commandment demand of us?**

We must respect God's gift of life in ourselves and in others. 2259

**204. How do we sin against the fifth commandment?**

We sin against the fifth commandment by murder, suicide, abortion, wanton violence, scandal and revenge. 2268ff

**205. What is murder?**

Murder is the wilful and unjust taking of human life.

**206. Why is abortion gravely wrong?**

Because the unborn child is innocent and possesses a life given by God with full human rights and called to be with God forever. (cf D 2,2) (GS 51) 2270

**207. What are the duties of doctors and nurses in cases of difficult childbirth?**

The duties of doctors and nurses in such cases are to apply all medical skill to save the lives of both mother and child.

**208. Why is euthanasia gravely wrong?**

Because it is the direct ending of one's own or another's life. 2277

**209. Does the Church condemn abortion, and euthanasia?**

The Church does condemn abortion and euthanasia as gravely contrary to the moral law of God. (GS 51) 2270ff 2276

**210. What has Christ said about the need to avoid giving scandal?**

He has said: 'Whoever causes one of these little ones who believe in me to sin; it would be better for him to have a great millstone fastened round his neck and to be drowned in the depth of the sea.' (Matthew 18,6; Mark 9,42; Luke 17,2) 2284ff

**211. Why is direct sterilisation sinful?**

Because it is a grave mutilation which deprives the body of the power of either begetting or bearing children. 2297

**212. What is the Church's attitude to war?**

The Church works to end war which is the result of sin, because all men are brethren and God is their common father: 'Blessed are the peacemakers for they shall be called sons of God.' (Matthew 5,9) (GS 82) 2307

**213. Is the arms race necessary?**

The arms race is not necessary and is one of the greatest curses on the human race because it tends to bring about what it claims to prevent: 'All who take the sword will perish by the sword.' (Matthew 26,52) (GS 81) 2315

**214. Can a country defend itself?**

A country can defend itself to preserve its security and freedom, but it cannot use indiscriminate means of retaliation. (GS 79) 2309

## 6th and 9th Commandments: The Place of Sex within Marriage

**215. What are the sixth and ninth commandments?**

The sixth commandment is 'You shall not commit adultery' and the ninth commandment is 'You shall not covet your neighbour's wife'.

**216. What do the sixth and ninth commandments demand of us?**

We must be pure and modest in our behaviour: 'Blessed are the pure in heart, for they shall see God.' (Matthew, 5,8) 2518

**217. What is adultery?**

Adultery is the sin of unfaithfulness with another man or woman. 2380–1

**218. Why do these commandments also forbid impure thoughts?**

Because Jesus said: 'Everyone who looks at a woman lustfully has already committed adultery with her in his heart . . . All these evil things come from within, and they defile a man.' (Matthew 5,28; Mark 7,23) 2336

**219. Why are premarital sex and masturbation forbidden?**

Because the gift of sex can only be used within married love which alone is holy and creative. 2351ff

**220. What is the Church's attitude to homosexual acts?**

The Church considers that sexual relations between persons of the same sex are of their very nature seriously wrong. Homosexuals living a chaste life are called to holiness in the Church. (PH 8) 2357

**221. How must the Christian preserve purity?**

He must preserve purity by overcoming impure desires and temptations with God's grace, and by avoiding occasions of sin such as drugs, excessive drink, pornography and indecent entertainment. 2291
(Gal 5,16; 1 Thes 4,4) 2520

## 7th and 10th Commandments: Respect for the Possessions of Others

**222. What are the seventh and tenth commandments?**

The seventh commandment is: 'You shall not steal' and the tenth commandment is 'You shall not covet anything that belongs to your neighbour.'

**223. What do these commandments demand of us?**

We must respect the rights and possessions of others and not be consumed with envy for them, 'for we have crucified the flesh with its passions and desires'. (Gal 5,24) 2358

**224. How do we sin against the seventh commandment?**

We sin against the seventh commandment by deliberately defrauding people of what is theirs whether by vandalism, theft or dishonesty.

**225. Are we obliged to restore what we have stolen?**

We are strictly obliged to restitution of stolen goods, and we are not allowed to accept what has been stolen. (Eph 4,28) 2409f

**226. Have we a duty to respect the environment?**

We should have a great respect for the whole of creation because it has been given to those who are created in the image of God to take care of it. (Gen 2,15) (GS 37 CA 37) 2415ff

**227. How can we regard private ownership?**

Private ownership can be regarded as an extension of human freedom as well as an incentive to work, but not in isolation from the common good. (CA 31; GS 71) 2402ff

**228. Has everyone the right to a share of the earth's riches?**

Everyone has a right to possess a sufficient share of the earth's riches, because God destined the earth and its riches for all. (GS 69) 1905

**229. Have we a duty to help the poor?**

We have a duty to help the poor for as it says in the Gospels 'our abundance should supply their need' (2 Corinthians 8,14) and 'as you did it to one of the least of these my brethren, you did it to me.' (Matthew 25,40) (AA 8) 2443ff

**230. What should be our attitude to material possessions?**

We should use our possessions to 'lay up for ourselves treasures in heaven' (cf. Matthew 6,20) and not allow them to possess us. (GS 27) 2544ff

**231. How should we regard work?**

Work should be regarded as natural to man. Through the efforts involved, we receive a creative share in the redemption which Christ began in his work at Nazareth. (GS 34) 2427

**232. What is the duty of an employer?**

An employer must give his employees a just wage and provide fair working conditions. (cf. James 5,4) (GS 66) 2432

**233. What is a just wage?**

A just wage is one which allows a man to provide a decent livelihood for himself and his family. (GS 26; CA34) 2434

**234. What are the duties of an employee?**

An employee is bound to respect his employer's property, make good use of his time and give fair work for fair wages and conditions. (GS 43) 2411

**235. Have men a right to form Trade Unions?**

Men have a fundamental right to form Trade Unions which will represent their views to employers and involve them in management, as well as help to improve their working conditions. (G S 68) 2430

# X
# FULFILMENT IN CHRIST

**236. What are the two great commandments of Jesus Christ?**

The two great commandments of Jesus Christ are: 'You shall love the Lord Your God with all your heart and with all your soul and with all your strength and with all your mind.' and 'You shall love your neighbour as yourself.' (Mark 12, 30–31)

**237. Can we love God without loving our fellow men?**

It is impossible to love God without loving our fellow men for 'If anyone says, 'I love God' and hates his brother, he is a liar.' (I John 4,20) 2196

**238. Is it possible to live a perfect life?**

The Saints are abiding proof that in every age it is possible to answer the call of Christ: 'You must be perfect as Your heavenly Father is perfect.' (Matthew 5,48) (LG 40) 2012

**239. What is the Christian attitude to evil?**

There is only one ultimate evil and that is sin, from which we ask God to deliver us. (Matthew 6, 13) 2846

**240. What is the Christian attitude to suffering and death?**

We should accept suffering and death when they come because in them we are united more perfectly with Christ who took up his Cross for love of us.
(I Peter 2,21) 1010ff

## The Life after Death

**241. What happens after death?**

After death we must all come into the presence of Christ our judge, 'so that each one may receive good or evil, according to what he has done.'
(2 Corinthians 5,10)
(LG 48) 1038

**242. How will Christ judge those who die without perfect love of God?**

Those who die without perfect love of God will be purified in love in purgatory. 1030ff

**243. How do we know that there is a purgatory?**

We know that there is a purgatory because those who imperfectly love God when they die, do not deserve Hell nor are they worthy enough for heaven; we also know from the Church's constant teaching about the value of prayers for those in purgatory.
(LG 49) 1030

**244. How do we know that our prayers help those in purgatory?**

We know from the words of the Bible that 'it is a holy and pious thought to pray for the dead that they might be delivered from their sins.' (2 Maccabees 12,45). For this reason the Church sets aside the month of November for a time of special prayer for those in purgatory, and allows indulgences to be applied to the Holy Souls. (LG 50ff)

**245. How will Christ judge those who die in hatred of God?**

He will judge them worthy of the eternal punishment of hell. (LG 48) 1033ff

**246. How can an infinitely good God allow hell to exist?**

The infinitely good God allows angels and men to choose to be with him or to be separated from his love, for he is also infinitely just. 1037

**247. What do we mean by the resurrection of the body?**

We mean that all will rise again in the body at the last day.

**248. How do we know that all will rise again?**

We know from the fact of Christ's own resurrection – 'the first fruit of those who have fallen asleep' – (I Corinthians 15,20) and from his own promise: 'he who eats my Flesh and drinks my Blood has eternal life and I will raise him up at the last day.' (John 6,54) 'The resurrection from the dead is the assurance of Christians'. (RC 1,1) 988ff

**249. Will Christ come again on the last day?**

Christ will come again in power and majesty when this world comes to an end to deliver creation to his Father and overcome sin and death forever. (I Cor 15,24) (LG 51) 1047ff

**250. What is the glory and happiness of heaven?**

The glory and happiness of heaven is to see, love and enjoy God the Father through his Son in the Holy Spirit for ever. (I Cor 2:9) 'There we shall rest and we shall behold, we shall behold and we shall love, we shall love and we shall praise. This is what shall be in the end without end.' (CG 22,30,1)

# CATHOLIC PRAYERS

## 1. General Prayers

### The Sign of the Cross

*In the name of the Father, and of the Son, and of the Holy Spirit. Amen.*

### Our Father

*Our Father, who art in heaven, hallowed be Thy name; Thy kingdom come; Thy will be done on earth as it is in heaven. Give us this day our daily bread; and forgive us our trespasses as we forgive those who trespass against us; and lead us not into temptation, but deliver us from evil. Amen.*

### Glory be to the Father

*Glory be to the Father, and to the Son, and to the Holy Spirit. As it was in the beginning, is now, and ever shall be, world without end. Amen.*

### I Believe (The Apostles' Creed)

*I believe in God, the Father almighty, creator of heaven and earth. I believe in Jesus Christ, his only Son, our Lord. He was conceived by the power of the Holy Spirit and born of the Virgin Mary. He suffered under Pontius Pilate, was crucified, died, and was buried. He descended to the dead. On the third day he rose again. He ascended into heaven, and is seated at the right hand of the Father. He will come again to judge the living and the dead. I believe in the Holy Spirit, the holy Catholic Church, the communion of saints, the forgiveness of sins, the resurrection of the body, and the life everlasting. Amen*

### An Act of Contrition

*O my God, because you are so good, I am very sorry that I have sinned against you and by the help of your grace I will not sin again.*

### Prayer to the Holy Spirit

*Come, Holy Spirit, fill the hearts of your faithful and kindle in them the fire of your love. Send forth your Spirit and they shall be created. And you shall renew the face of the earth.*

Let us Pray:

*O God, you have taught the hearts of the faithful by the light of the Holy Spirit; grant that by the gift of the same Spirit, we may be always truly wise and ever rejoice in his consolation. Through Christ Our Lord. Amen.*

## 2. Morning and Evening Prayers

### A Morning Offering

*O Jesus, through the most pure heart of Mary, I offer you all my prayers, works, sufferings and joys of this day, for all the intentions of your Divine Heart in the Holy Mass.*

*O angel of God, appointed by Divine mercy to be my guardian, enlighten and protect, direct and govern me this day. Amen.*

## Evening Prayers

*O my God, I adore you, and I love you with all my heart. I thank you for having created me and saved me by your grace, and for having preserved me during this day. I pray that you will take for yourself whatever good I may have done this day and that you will forgive me whatever evil I have done. Protect me this night, and may your grace be with me always and with those I love. Amen.*

*O my God, as I came from you, as I am made through you, as I live in you, so may I at last return to you and be with you for ever. Through Christ Our Lord. Amen.*

*Jesus, Mary and Joseph, I give you heart and my soul Jesus, Mary and Joseph, assist me in my last agony. Jesus, Mary and Joseph, may I breathe forth my soul in peace with you.*

### 3. Prayers during the day

## An Act of Faith

*My God, I believe in you and all that your Church teaches, because you have said it, and your word is true.*

## An Act of Hope

*My God, I hope in you, for grace and for glory, because of your promises, your mercy and your power.*

## An Act of Charity

*My God, because you are so good, I love you with all my heart, and for your sake, I love my neighbour as myself.*

## Prayer before work or study

*Almighty God, be the beginning and end of all we do and say. Prompt our actions with your grace and complete them with your all powerful help. Through Christ Our Lord. Amen.*

## Prayers of Dedication

*Teach us, good Lord, to serve you as you deserve; to give and not to count the cost; to fight and not to heed the wounds; to toil and not to seek for rest; to labour and to ask for no reward, save that of knowing that we do your will. Through Christ Our Lord. Amen*

(St Ignatius of Loyola 1491–1556)

*The things, good Lord, that I pray for, give me the grace to labour for.*

(St Thomas More 1478–1535)

## Prayer for Vocations

*O Lord Jesus Christ, who has chosen the Apostles and their successors, the bishops and priests of the Catholic Church, to preach the true faith throughout the whole world, we earnestly beseech you to choose from among us, priests and religious brothers and sisters, who will gladly spend their entire lives to make you better known and loved. Amen.*

## Prayer for the Pope

*O God, eternal shepherd of your people, look with love on N. our Pope, your appointed successor to St Peter on whom you built your Church. May he be the source and foundation of our communion in faith and love. Through Christ Our Lord. Amen.*

(Roman Missal, Votive Mass for the Pope)

## Prayer before a Crucifix

*Behold, O good and most sweet Jesus, I kneel before you and with all the ardour of my soul, I pray and beseech you to engrave deep and vivid impressions of faith, hope, and charity upon my heart, with true repentance for my sins, and a very firm resolve to make amends. Meanwhile I ponder over your five wounds, dwelling upon them with deep compassion and grief, and recalling the words that the prophet David long ago put into your mouth, good Jesus, concerning yourself: 'They have pierced my hands and my feet; they have counted all my bones.'*

XV Cent.

## Prayer before the Blessed Sacrament

*My Lord and my God, I firmly believe that you are here; that you hear me and you see me. I adore you with profound reverence and I ask pardon for my sins.*

## Prayer after Holy Communion (The Anima Christi)

*Soul of Christ, sanctify me.*
*Body of Christ, save me.*
*Blood of Christ, inebriate me.*
*Water from the side of Christ, wash me.*
*Passion of Christ, strengthen me.*
*O good Jesus, hear me.*
*Within your wounds, hide me.*
*Never permit me to be separated from you.*
*From the wicked enemy defend me.*
*In the hour of my death call me*
*And bid me come to you*
*That with your saints, I may praise you*
*For ever and ever. Amen.*

Ascribed to Pope John XXII († 1334)

## The Divine Praises

*Blessed be God.*
*Blessed be His Holy Name.*
*Blessed be Jesus Christ, true God and true Man.*
*Blessed be the Name of Jesus.*
*Blessed be His most Sacred Heart.*
*Blessed be His Most Precious Blood.*
*Blessed be Jesus in the Most Holy Sacrament of the Altar.*
*Blessed be the Holy Spirit, the Paraclete.*
*Blessed be the great Mother of God, Mary most holy.*
*Blessed be her holy and Immaculate Conception.*
*Blessed be her glorious Assumption.*
*Blessed be the name of Mary, Virgin and Mother.*
*Blessed be St Joseph, her spouse most chaste.*
*Blessed be God in His Angels and in His saints.*

## Grace before meals

*Bless us, O Lord, and these your gifts which we are about to receive from your bounty. Through Christ Our Lord. Amen.*

## Grace after meals

*We give you thanks, almighty God, for these and all your benefits, who live and reign, for ever and ever. Amen.*

# 4. Prayers to Our Lady

## Hail Mary

*Hail Mary, full of grace, the Lord is with thee; blessed art thou among women, and blessed is the fruit of thy womb Jesus. Holy Mary, Mother of God, pray for us sinners, now, and at the hour of our death. Amen.*

## Hail Holy Queen

*Hail Holy Queen, mother of mercy; hail our life, our sweetness, and our hope! To thee do we cry, poor banished children of Eve; to thee do we send up our sighs, mourning and weeping in this vale of tears. Turn then, most gracious advocate, thine eyes of mercy towards us; and after this our exile, show unto us the blessed fruit of thy womb, Jesus. O clement, O loving, O sweet Virgin Mary.*
*Pray for us, O holy Mother of God*
*That we may be made worthy of the promises of Christ.*

## The Memorare

*Remember, O most loving Virgin Mary, that it is a thing unheard of, that anyone ever had recourse to your protection, implored your help, or sought your intercession, and was left forsaken. Filled therefore with confidence in your goodness I fly to you, O Mother, Virgin of virgins. To you I come, before you I stand, a sorrowful sinner. Despise not my poor words, O Mother of the Word of God, but graciously hear and grant my prayer.*

## Prayer for Our Lady's Protection

*We fly to thy protection, O holy Mother of God, despise not our petitions in our necessities, but deliver us from all dangers, O ever glorious and blessed Virgin.*

III Cent.

## The Rosary

## The Joyful Mysteries

'Behold I bring you news of great joy'. (Luke 2,10)

1. *The Annunciation Our Father . . . Ten Hail Marys. Glory be . . .*

2. *The Visitation*
3. *The Birth of Our Lord*
4. *The Presentation of Jesus in the Temple*
5. *The Finding of Jesus in the Temple.*

## The Sorrowful Mysteries

'He has surely borne our griefs and carried our sorrows'. (Isaiah 53,4)

1. *The Agony of Jesus in the Garden*
2. *The Scourging at the Pillar*
3. *The Crowning with thorns*
4. *Jesus carries His Cross*
5. *The Crucifixion.*

## The Glorious Mysteries

'God has highly exalted Him and bestowed on Him the name which is above every name.' (Philippians 2,9)

1. *The Resurrection*
2. *The Ascension*
3. *The Descent of the Holy Spirit on Our Lady and the apostles*
4. *The Assumption*
5. *The Coronation of Our Lady in heaven.*

*Hail, Holy Queen . . .* *(see beginning of section)*

Let us pray:

*O God, whose only begotten Son, by His life, death and resurrection has purchased for us the rewards of eternal life; grant, we beseech thee, that meditating upon these mysteries in the most holy rosary of the Blessed Virgin Mary, we may both imitate what they contain and obtain what they promise. Through Christ Our Lord. Amen.*

## The Angelus

– a prayer which sanctifies 'the characteristic periods of the day – morning, noon and evening – and constitutes an invitation to pause in prayer' (Marialis Cultus 1974 n 41)

*The angel of the Lord declared unto Mary*
*R/ And she conceived by the Holy Spirit. Hail Mary . . .*

*Behold the handmaid of the Lord*
*R /Be it done to me according to your word.*
*Hail Mary . . .*

*The Word was made flesh*
*R/ And dwelt among us.* *Hail Mary . . .*

*Pray for us, O holy Mother of God*
*R/ That we may be made worthy of the promises of Christ*

Let us pray:

*Pour forth, we beseech you, O Lord, your grace into our hearts, that we to whom the Incarnation of Christ your Son was made known by the message of an angel, may, by his Passion and Cross, be brought to the glory of his Resurrection. Through Christ Our Lord. Amen.*

## Regina Caeli
(recited in place of the Angelus during Eastertide)

*Queen of heaven, rejoice! Alleluia.*
*For he whom you merited to bear, Alleluia.*
*Has risen, as he said. Alleluia.*
*Pray for us to God. Alleluia.*

*V. Rejoice and be glad, O Virgin Mary, Alleluia.*
*R/ For the Lord has risen indeed. Alleluia.*

Let us pray:

*O God, who through the resurrection of your Son,*
*Our Lord Jesus Christ, willed to fill the world with joy,*
*grant, we beseech you, that through his Virgin Mother,*
*Mary, we may come to the joys of everlasting life.*
*Through the same Christ Our Lord. Amen*

## 5. Prayers for the Faithful Departed

### The De Profundis (Psalm 130)

*Out of the depths, I have cried to you, O Lord.*
*Lord, hear my voice.*
*Let your ears be attentive.*
*To the voice of my supplication.*
*If you, O Lord, shall observe iniquities,*
*Lord, who shall endure it?*
*For with you there is merciful forgiveness;*
*And by reason of your law, I have waited for you,*
*O Lord.*
*My soul has relied on his word;*
*My soul has hoped in the Lord*
*From the morning watch even until night*
*Let Israel hope in the Lord.*
*Because with the Lord there is mercy*
*And with him plentiful redemption.*
*And He shall redeem Israel*
*from all his iniquities.*

### Prayers for deceased relatives and friends

*Almighty Father, source of forgiveness and salvation, grant that our relatives and friends who have passed from this life, may, through the intercession of the Blessed Virgin Mary and of all the saints, come to share your eternal happiness. Through Christ Our Lord. Amen.*

## Prayer for a happy death

*O Lord, support us all the day long until the shadows lengthen and the evening comes and the busy world is hushed and the fever of life is over, and our work is done. Then, Lord, in your mercy, grant us a safe lodging, a holy rest, and peace at the last. Amen.*

Cardinal Newman (1801–1890)

*Eternal Rest grant to them, O Lord*
*And let perpetual light shine upon them. May they rest in peace. Amen*

*May the souls of the faithful departed, through the mercy of God rest in peace. Amen.*

*May the Lord bless us, may he keep us from all evil and bring us to life everlasting. Amen.*

# INDEX